THRILLING THEME PARKS

# DOLLYWOOD

BY MONIKA DAVIES

EPIC

EPIC, AN IMPRINT OF BELLWETHER MEDIA BY FLUTTERBEE

# EPIC

**EPIC BOOKS** are no ordinary books. They burst with intense action, high-speed heroics, and shadows of the unknown. Are you ready for an Epic adventure?

This edition first published in 2027 by Bellwether Media, Inc.



For information regarding permission, write to Bellwether Media, Inc., Attention: Permissions Department, 3500 American Blvd W, Suite 150, Bloomington, MN 55431.

Library of Congress Cataloging-in-Publication Data

Names: Davies, Monika author
Title: Dollywood / by Monika Davies.
Description: Epic. | Minneapolis, Minnesota : Bellwether Media, Inc, 2027. | Series: Thrilling theme parks | Includes bibliographical references and index. | Audience: Ages 8-12 | Audience: Grades 4-6 | Summary: "Engaging images accompany information about Dollywood. The combination of high-interest subject matter and light text is intended for students in grades 2 through 7"-- Provided by publisher.
Identifiers: LCCN 2026013870 (print) | LCCN 2026013871 (ebook) | ISBN 9798898801021 library binding | ISBN 9798898802264 ebook
Subjects: LCSH: Dollywood (Pigeon Forge, Tenn.) | Parton, Dolly | Amusement parks--Tennessee
Classification: LCC GV1853.3.T22 D38 2027 (print) | LCC GV1853.3.T22 (ebook)
LC record available at https://lccn.loc.gov/2026013870
LC ebook record available at https://lccn.loc.gov/2026013871

Editor: Elizabeth Neuenfeldt Designer: Gabriel Hilger

Printed in the United States of America, North Mankato, MN.

# TABLE OF CONTENTS

# LOVE EVERY MOMENT

A string band plays. A banjo twangs. The singers sing together.

A family sits in the front row. They spent all morning on rides. Now, they tap their feet to the beat. What a memorable day at Dollywood!

Dollywood is a **theme park** near the Great Smoky Mountains. It is in Pigeon Forge, Tennessee.

# DOLLYWOOD MAP

The park has over 50 rides and **attractions**. It is also has live music!

# THE MAKING OF DOLLYWOOD

Dollywood started as a park called Rebel Railroad. The park opened in 1961.

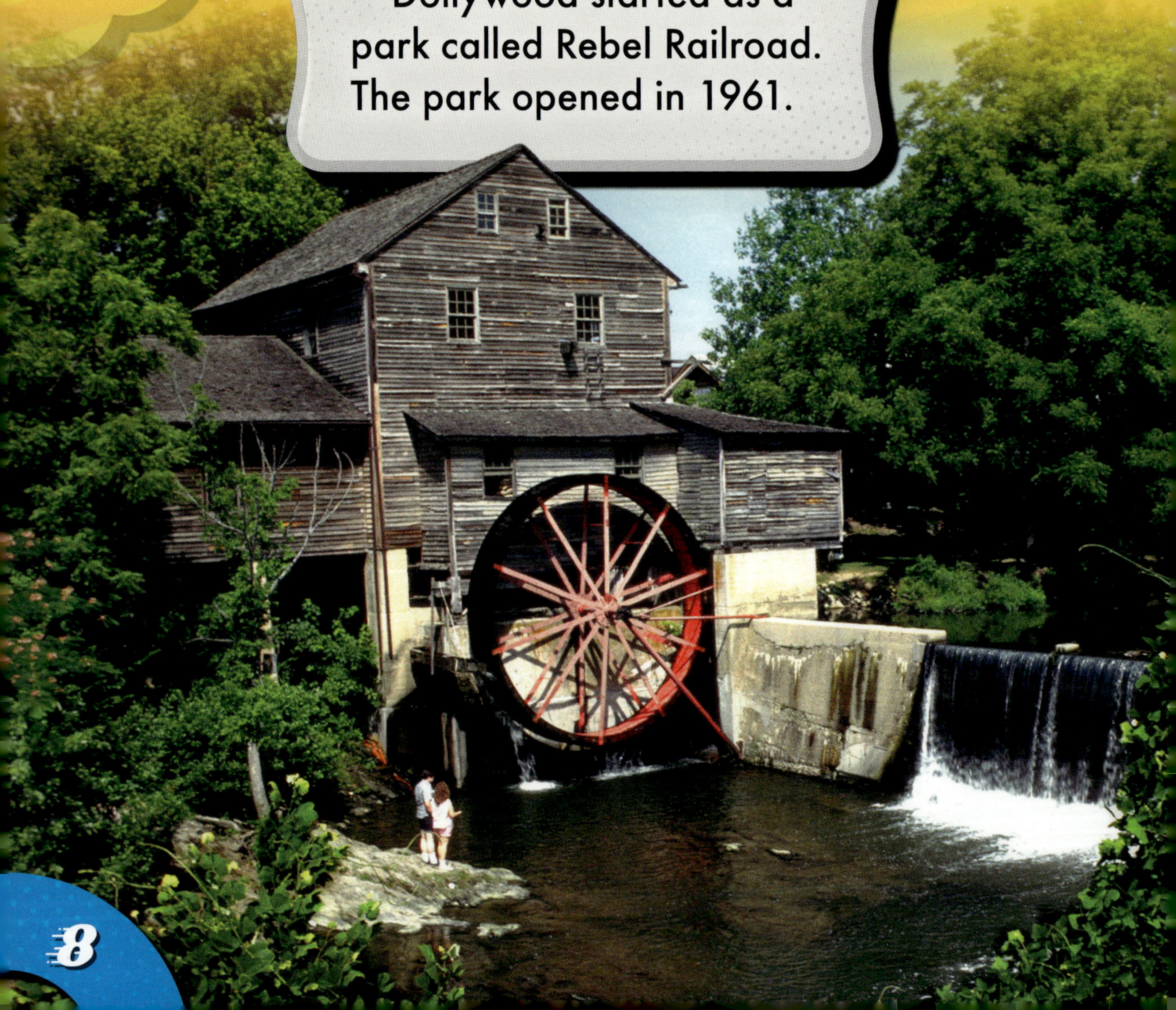

**CLASSIC COASTER**

Blazing Fury opened in 1978. It is a coaster that shares a story about a terrible fire. People still ride it today!

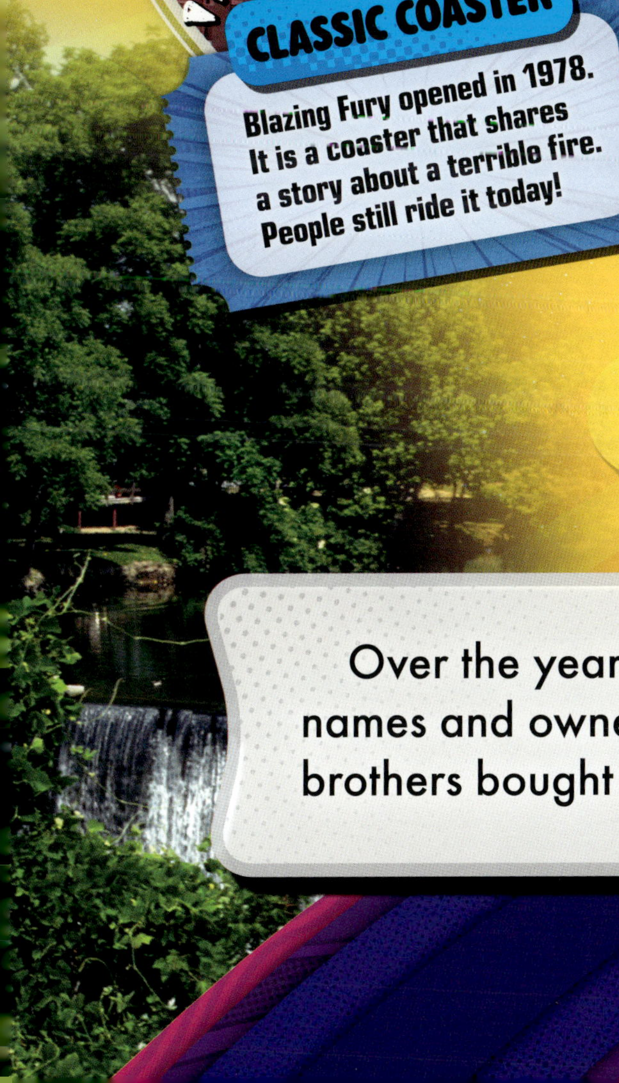

Over the years, the park changed names and owners. The Herschend brothers bought the park in 1977.

Dolly Parton is a country singer. She was born in the Great Smoky Mountains. In the 1980s, she had an idea. She wanted a theme park near her hometown.

# DOLLY PARTON

**BORN** 1946

**ROLE** Co-owner of Dollywood

**ACCOMPLISHMENT** Helped Dollywood grow

The Herschend brothers heard her idea. They met Dolly. They became partners!

REPLICA OF DOLLY'S CHILDHOOD HOME

Dollywood opened on May 3, 1986. It had four themed areas. It also had a **replica** of Dolly's childhood home.

Dolly sang **ads** to **promote** the park. More people visited the park.

## NO RIDES FOR DOLLY

Dolly never rides the park's rides! She feels sick when she rides roller coasters.

The park grew. Eagle Mountain **Sanctuary** opened in 1991. Visitors can see bald eagles up close.

Tennessee Tornado opened in 1999. Riders go in loops on this speedy coaster!

EAGLE MOUNTAIN SANCTUARY

# Dollywood Attendance Records

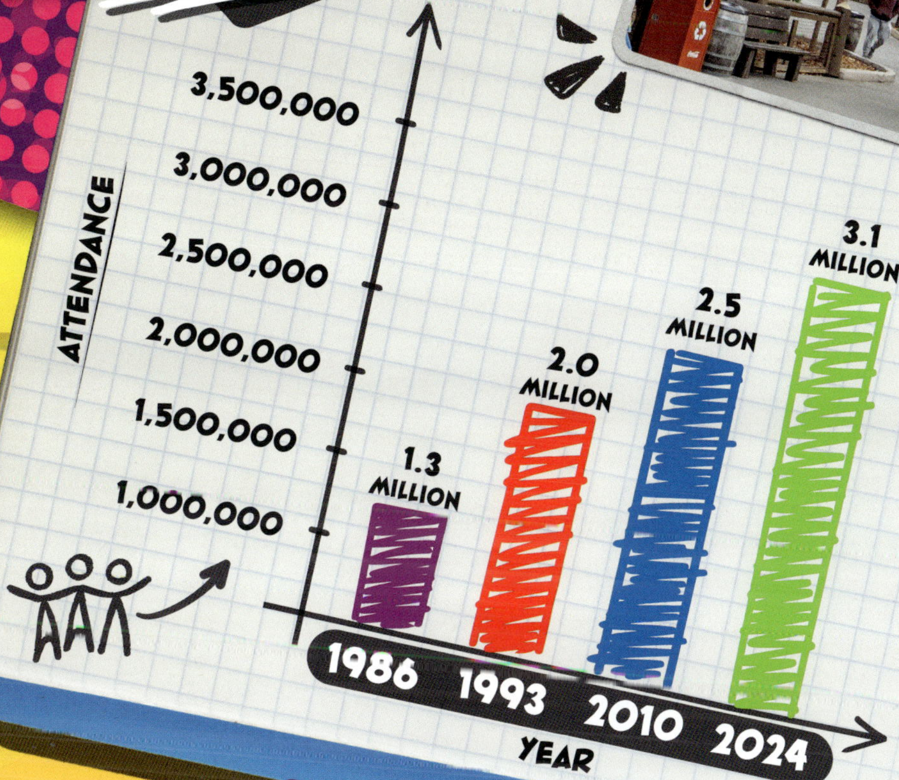

TENNESSEE TORNADO

# DOLLYWOOD TODAY

**ALL ABOARD!**

The Dollywood Express is a 20-minute train ride. Riders get great views of the park and the nearby mountains!

Dollywood has 11 themed areas. Families can view the park from Treetop Tower in Wildwood Grove.

The Dollywood Express rolls out from the Village area. Cinnamon bread is served in Craftsman's Valley.

Live music plays on Showstreet. The Dolly Parton Experience is in Jukebox Junction. It opened in 2024. It honors Dolly's life story.

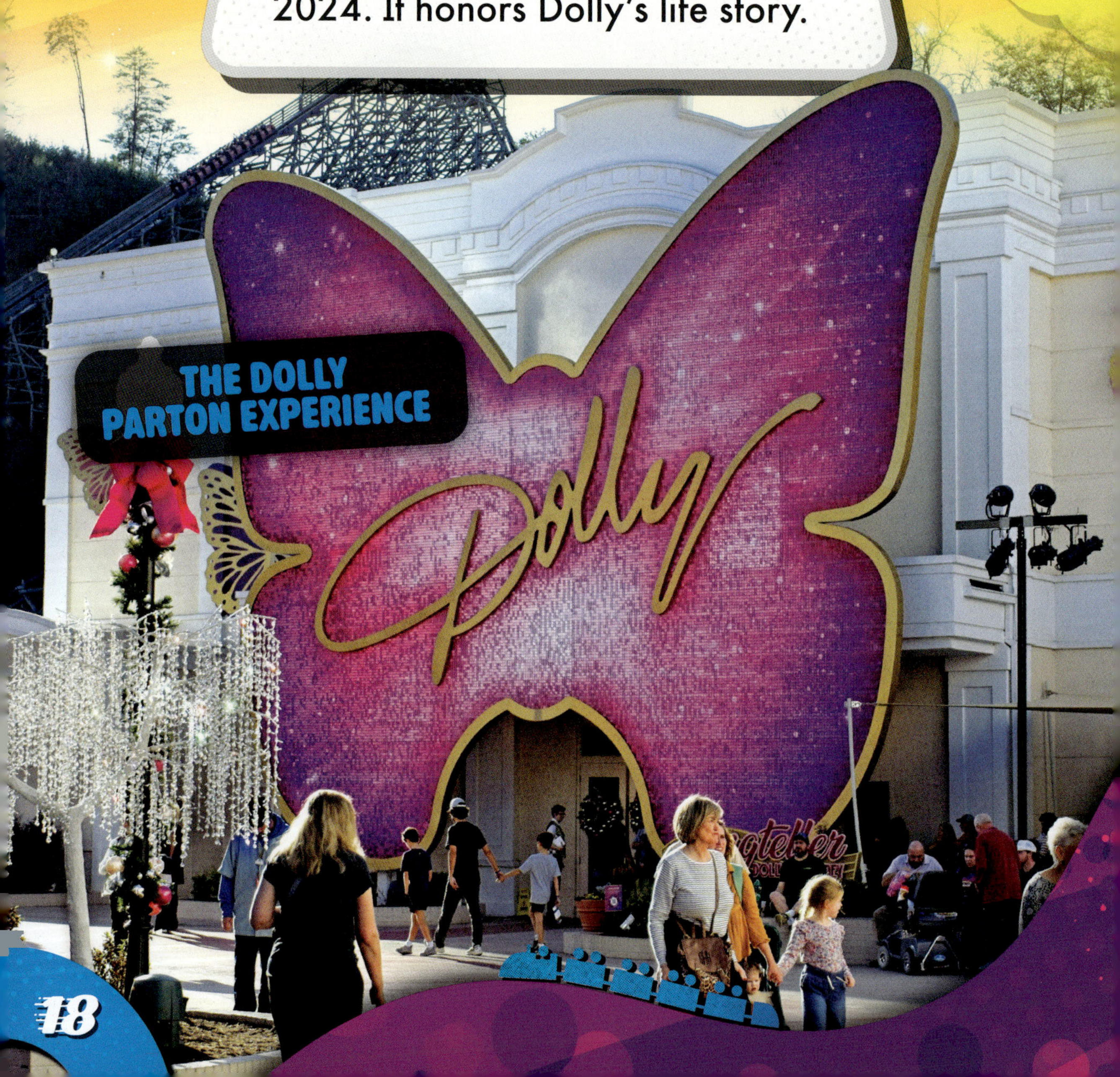


THE DOLLY PARTON EXPERIENCE

Nightflight Expedition was announced in 2025. It is a boat ride and roller coaster!

## LIGHTNING ROD

**WHAT IS IT?**

A fast roller coaster made of wood and steel

**STAT**

It has a 165-foot (50.3-meter) drop.

**FUN FACT**

Its cars are based on 1950s hot rod cars.

# Dollywood Events

Dollywood hosts the I Will Always Love You Music Festival in the spring. People sing along to fun shows.

## Smoky Mountain Christmas

**DATE**

November to early January

**EVENT**

Visitors view holiday lights and listen to music.

Visitors collect butterfly magnets, bags, and more. Dollywood is full of joy and fun!

# Glossary

**ads**—notices and messages that tell people to do or buy things

**attractions**—interesting things that people want to see or visit

**promote**—to make something more popular or better known

**replica**—a close copy of something

**sanctuary**—a place that provides protection or shelter

**theme park**—a park where the rides and shows are based on a certain subject

# To Learn More

## AT THE LIBRARY

Davies, Monika. *Six Flags.* Minneapolis, Minn.: Bellwether Media, 2027.

Rathburn, Betsy. *Dolly Parton.* Minneapolis, Minn.: Bellwether Media, 2026.

Romero, Libby. *Amusement Park.* New York, N.Y.: DK Publishing, 2023.

## ON THE WEB

**FACTSURFER**

Factsurfer.com gives you a safe, fun way to find more information.

1. Go to www.factsurfer.com.

2. Enter "Dollywood" into the search box and click 🔍.

3. Select your book cover to see a list of related content.

# Index




The images in this book are reproduced through the courtesy of: imageBROKER.com/ Alamy Stock Photo, front cover, p. 1; AFF/ Alamy Stock Photo, front cover, pp. 1, 2-3, 3, 10 (inset), 20, 21; Jaclyn Vernace, front cover, pp. 1, 14; GTCRFOTO/ Alamy Stock Photo, pp. 4, 5, 16-17; Castle Light Images/ Alamy Stock Photo, p. 6; Chad Robertson Media, p. 7; imac, p. 8; Jeremy Thompson/ Wikimedia Commons, p. 9; Emma Stoner/ Alamy Stock Photo, p. 10; jharsh21, p. 11; The TN collection/ Alamy Stock Photo, pp. 12, 14 (inset); Ron Davis/ Contributor/ Getty Images, p. 13; DollyFanJoie/ Wikimedia Commons, p. 15 (Tennessee Tornado); RaisaMacouzet, pp. 15 (attendance), 17; Lee Lawson/ Alamy Stock Photo, p. 18; UCG/ Contributor/ Getty Images, p. 19 (Lightning Rod); Nicole Weaver/ Alamy Stock Photo, p. 19 (sign).